# Smart Moves

PRITCHETT & ASSOCIATES, INC.
*Dallas, Texas*

# Which is Easier– Making the Deal, or Making the Deal Work?

While you wrestle with that question for a minute, think about how much money is at stake. Then consider the number of people in the two companies...all the careers that are involved...the lives you're playing with here. You might also reflect on how all the other stakeholders are watching intently–your customers, suppliers, bankers, the public who owns your stock. And, of course, the press may be hanging around just aching for a hot story about how things are going wrong. Your competition would love to make a field day out of this.

Obviously there is a lot on the line here. The next few months aren't going to be a day at the beach.

It's interesting how a merger or acquisition is always based on a financial proposition. But once the papers are signed, success depends on management effectiveness. And no matter how well conceived the deal is, it's not a good one if management fails to make it work.

The integration strategy has to be right.

The timing has to be right.

The right people have to be put in the right places.

It's not enough to be busy–you have to be busy doing the *right things*. The situation is very unforgiving.

Now for the answer to the big question we asked at the beginning:
Out of every one hundred companies that cut a deal,
seventy-five get cut to shreds in the months that
follow. Making the deal is just a warmup...the real job
is making it work.

Frankly, there is no "school solution," but this booklet sketches out a set of ground rules that have dramatically improved our clients' odds for merger success. Pritchett and Associates has been consulting on merger integration strategy longer than anyone else in the world. We've learned a lot over the years about what works and what doesn't when companies are being acquired and merged. We'd like to think you can benefit from our experience.

Let us say this: You think swinging the deal was tough? The closing is just the beginning.

# Table of Contents

# Start Managing the Transition When the Deal is Announced.

Things begin changing in an organization as soon as your people learn that a deal is in the works. The possibility that they might be acquired and merged causes people to think and act differently. A new set of organizational dynamics comes into play immediately. Attitudinal shifts and a new set of employee concerns can alter the corporate climate significantly.

It's a mistake to assume that the transition period starts when the deal is closed, when the papers are finally signed. Weeks and even months can go by before the merger/acquisition is finalized. Due diligence work, regulatory approval, and the negotiation process itself can drag things out for a long time.

Problems, however, don't wait around on management to close the deal.

So transition management should begin immediately when the deal is announced. Otherwise, you're going to be running behind, and the bulk of your time will be spent trying to fix problems rather than prevent them. You'll get caught in a cross-fire–on one hand needing to develop your integration strategy, and on the other hand having to deal with problems that have a headstart on you.

A wait-and-see attitude puts you and the organization at a severe disadvantage. You'll end up being reactive, instead of proactive. Rather than being effectively positioned to *shape* circumstances, you'll be a *victim* of them.

But what if the deal falls through? What if the merger/acquisition event never materializes? Would that mean a lot of wasted effort gearing up for nothing?

No.

The organization is jittery. Off balance. Destabilized. People are hyper-alert, maybe shaken out of their routines, and primed for change. There's extra work to be done—you may need to settle things down, or perhaps you should seize the opportunity to make changes and torque up organizational performance.

But it's not going to be business as usual.

# Protect Productivity.

The merger is a major distraction for your people. It interferes with their work focus and undermines job commitment. This, plus the destabilization that is simply generic to mergers, causes productivity to take a damaging hit during the transition period.

Our experience indicates that employee productivity in a newly acquired or merged company gets cut in half during the first several months of a transition period. Some companies do better than this, of course, but almost always there is a sharp decline in productivity during the early stages.

Sagging productivity would be enough of a problem, but it leads to a secondary dilemma: failure feeds on itself. When employees see obvious slippage in organizational momentum, they often interpret that as evidence that it's a "bad merger" or that top management is doing a poor job of handling the situation.

Interestingly, the destabilization caused by a merger powerfully increases the energy level in a company. But unless that energy gets channeled along productive lines, it's a destructive force that can sabotage corporate effectiveness.

There are several ground rules for coping:
• Operate with very short-range goals or objectives.
• Initiate new, merger-specific incentive programs for the transition period.
• Monitor performance more closely.
• Provide employees quick, accurate feedback regarding shortfalls in their performance effectiveness.

• Move quickly to clarify roles and responsibilities for each employee.
• Pass out more "psychological paychecks" to your people.
• Even though you may secretly be expecting less from your people, ask for more. Actually raise the performance standards.

Just as failure feeds on itself, success breeds success. So keep the pressure on to protect, even enhance, productivity levels.

# Tighten up the Integration Period Time Frame.

The most common complaint employees have in the typical merger sounds like this:

"Nothing's happening...
Why don't they get on with it?...
They're moving too slowly."

Instinctively, the employees seem to know what's best. Certainly they know what they want, and that is for top management to get the merger over and done with instead of letting it drag on and on.

Employees need answers. They want closure. What they can't stand is "not knowing," and having to continue working in an atmosphere of uncertainty and destabilization.

A lengthy, slowly paced integration is a high-risk strategy. Such an approach exposes the organization for a longer period to the damage that can be done by generic organizational problems brought on by a merger.

It's worth noting that approximately seven out of ten mergers are either disappointments or outright failures. And the *average* merger transition spans about twenty-four months, usually *twice* the time that should be allotted.

We feel one of the key predictors of a merger's success or failure is the number of months it takes to move from start to finish – i.e., the length of the transition period. If there is to be a true merger, an actual consolidation of organizations, we typically push our clients to get it done within a nine to twelve month period. That alone dramatically raises the odds of merger success.

Frankly, you don't have time to take your time. If you do, problems will outrun you and productivity will drop through the floor (taking employee morale with it). As the saying goes, "Skate fast over thin ice."

# Control the Amount
# of Destabilization.

A merger always rocks the orga-
nizational boat. Sometimes it sinks. The job of management is to control
the destabilization so your ship stays afloat.

It's apparent there's no way you can avoid the upheaval when you
consider the underlying problems:

1. Resistance to change
2. Divided loyalties
3. Blurred roles and responsibilities
4. Unclear reporting relationships
5. Communication tangles
6. Power shifts
7. Job insecurity
8. Unusual employee turnover
9. Policy and procedure changes
10. Infighting

The best you can hope for is to contain the destabilization, to
minimize it as much as possible and get through the treacherous
water as quickly as you can.

Start out with a sophisticated, well-conceived, professionally
guided integration strategy. Make sure that both the *substance* and
*timing* of your integration plan are expertly designed, and ensure
that all in key management positions are aligned in supporting the
strategy.

The time to work through differences is on the front end, not
after the rollout of the integration plan has begun. Once a coherent
strategy has been designed and decided upon, either get the backing

of managers and executives or get rid of them. You can't afford to go forward struggling to deal day by day, week by week, with overt opposition or subtle sabotage.

Managing a merger is a big job. It's hard enough with everybody pulling together, and when people are pulling in different directions the chances for success grow slim.

You simply cannot afford to second-guess your strategy continually, or to keep starting over with a new one. Neither can you make it work if people are pursuing their own private strategies.

Of course, some fine-tuning and redirecting of your strategy is inevitable as the merger proceeds. You have to show some flexibility because you learn as you go, circumstances keep changing, and priorities shift. There is a lot of impromptu management that cannot be avoided.

But the integration process needs to be carefully structured and systematically managed in order to restabilize the firm. That's how you protect productivity, preserve your client base, and position the organization for future success.

We constantly see well-intentioned managers and executives about to pursue an integration approach that would inadvertently (1) add to or (2) prolong the destabilization. It's a tricky situation, and the *obvious* moves often are not the *smart* ones.

# Be Realistic About
# Cultural Differences.

One of the most common merger philosophies we hear goes like this:

"We're going to take our time, do it right, and form a new culture that represents the best of both worlds."

That sounds good in theory, but it's a high risk proposition. Our experience is that companies almost never pull it off successfully.

It makes about as much sense as a man and woman who marry and announce that they plan to blend their two personalities into one...50-50...at the same time that they're trying to adjust to all the routine stresses and strains of married life. It's a recipe for failure, whether you're talking about a marriage or a merger.

The "best of both worlds" strategy for integrating cultures brings traumatic destabilization to both organizations. Managers in both companies end up struggling to manage an unfamiliar situation. They can't necessarily draw on their previous successful experience as they wrestle with subtle and not-so-subtle ramifications of cultural shifts. Besides, after all is said and done, one of the two cultures virtually always comes out on top anyhow.

We recommend a much more pragmatic, business-oriented approach: integrate one company, not two. Usually the argument tilts in favor of going with the dominant or most financially successful culture. Be very clear and upfront with everybody about your plan. This makes the merger far less of a jarring experience for the firm whose culture prevails. Furthermore, it actually permits an easier transition for people in the other organization as well, if you take the following steps:

1. Pull no punches in explaining your integration strategy.
2. Try to identify the key differences in the two "corporate personalities."
3. Educate employees regarding what the new cultural realities will be.

No question, the people (from *both* organizations) need help if they are to understand how to operate comfortably within the confines of those cultural realities that will prevail. Otherwise it can take months for them to "break the code" and figure out how to handle themselves on the job.

We're not suggesting that you shouldn't come out of the merger with a better organization. Frankly, you should seize the window of opportunity the merger shakeup gives you to work toward a newer and better culture.

But remember–the key function of corporate culture is to bring stability to the organization, just as a key function of an individual's personality is to bring stability to the person. So you must question the wisdom in deliberately tearing *both* cultures apart now when there are so many other new pressure points brought on by the merger.

# Manage the Turnover.

**A** direct by-product of the merger/ acquisition process is an increase in employee turnover. It's a fact of life that, whether planned or not, there will be merger casualties.

Most of the time merging companies can survive operating with fewer people, but not fewer quality people. So you can't just sit back and let nature take its course so far as turnover is concerned.

Natural attrition during a merger produces a loss of good employees and minimal turnover among marginal, weak players. The reason for this is obvious–it's easy for good people to find new jobs, but much more difficult for the lesser talents to reposition themselves successfully elsewhere.

In most cases it's advantageous to consolidate and downsize. The financial logic driving the merger probably is based on the assumption that certain economies can be achieved through collapsing functions, eliminating redundancies, closing certain facilities, or doing away with some of the layers in the organizational hierarchy.

But too often top management announces that these personnel cutbacks will be achieved gradually through the normal attrition process–i.e., not replacing employees who quit.

One problem with that strategy is that it offers no hope for strengthening the organization. (As mentioned earlier, *talent* leaves first, not the deadwood.) Secondly, it's a sluggish approach–an uncontrolled process–which assumes mere passage of time will take care of the problem. That's not good management. It makes about as much sense as holding an employment lottery, where the composition of your workforce is left to chance.

Here are the ground rules you should follow:

1. *Always* operate with the assumption that there will be turnover which directly results from the merger.

2. Plan on taking advantage of the opportunity the merger presents to get rid of marginal employees.

3. Look for opportunities to consolidate and streamline for a more efficient organization.

4. Move rapidly to re-recruit your good employees.

It's much easier to succeed with a team comprised of quality players that you select deliberately rather than try to win a game with those who randomly show up to play. Take charge of the situation... make sure the new organization is staffed for success.

# Conduct the Necessary
# *Soft Due Diligence*.

**T**raditionally the merger due diligence process has focused on legal and financial issues – e.g., contractual matters, litigation points, economic and fiscal considerations, etc. Obviously that's an important exercise.

But when mergers fail, as they too frequently do, the odds are it reflects a sloppy job of *soft due diligence*. We coined that phrase to describe our work for clients in analyzing a number of factors critical to merger success, such as the following:

- Management strengths and weaknesses
- Organization structure and the needs/opportunities for redesign
- Salient differences in corporate culture that must be reconciled
- Organizational "soft spots" that could put the merger at risk

There is powerful logic in favor of systematically assessing the competencies of key players in the new organization. You should not automatically assume that people who have been successful in a pre-merger environment will perform with the same effectiveness under a new regime and in a different corporate setup. People's strengths often become weaknesses during a merger transition period.

It's not at all unusual for an individual to be an all-star in a slow, deliberate setup style offense, yet be a loser in a fast-break game. Ordinarily, the most staunch defenders of the old culture – i.e., the loyalists – have the most difficult struggle adjusting to the inevitable changes brought on by a merger.

This highlights the needs for an objective, professional appraisal of people's competencies and potential. An important part of the *soft due diligence* work involves identifying those individuals who can tolerate the ambiguity and uncertainty, facilitate the change process, take appropriate risks, communicate effectively, and generally enjoy the challenge of the merger with the opportunities it will provide.

The absence of such an assessment process practically guarantees the miscasting of people. It means that some poor souls are going to be set up for failure. A merger invariably creates a number of new jobs, and profoundly alters the requirements of many others. Often employees "inherit" positions, and end up in roles where they can't really measure up to the new demands. And when they can only run at half speed, or prove unable to "go the distance" in a merger, you can expect dangerous slippage in corporate effectiveness.

The other facets of *soft due diligence* provide the same high calibre insurance against nasty surprises as the merger unfolds. These analyses are the "ounce of prevention" that has a tremendous payback to your organization.

# Set Your Priorities Carefully.

**O**rdinarily managers and executives find it extremely difficult, particularly during the early stages of the merger transition period, to (1) establish priorities correctly and (2) stay focused on them.

You're particularly vulnerable to this problem if you start out with a poorly conceived or misdirected integration strategy. Rest assured, there will be more than enough "impromptu management" and improvising called for even when your integration plans are carefully made.

Another major cause of misplaced priorities comes in letting yourself respond to the last pressure point. Obviously, there will be many things pulling at you, vying for your time and attention as well as company resources. Everybody has his or her own private agenda... each employee wants a part of you. Problems seem to pop up everywhere, making a fresh set of demands on a manager's time. It's easy to get "scattered." Don't make the mistake of giving your time and attention to the person or problem that makes the most noise–volume is a very unreliable predictor of true priorities. You can easily slip into a firefighting mode, where you burn up precious energy and waste valuable time chasing tangents or concentrating on things that are "urgent" but not the most important.

Another trap lies in "seduction by the familiar." Managers frequently set priorities by default, spending the bulk of their time on what they have habitually done, like to do, or find to be the least distasteful. Your personal preferences will not be a good guide to the high priority moves during a merger. For example, we were brought in to consult on a merger where the new company president spent two precious weeks immediately after the deal was finalized chasing all over the United States visiting plant sites when he didn't even have an integration strategy framed out or a transition management group in place. Perhaps he took comfort in being visible and on the move. But there's a big difference between being busy and being focused on what counts the most.

The best guidelines for well-placed priorities are to concentrate on the things that:

1. Shorten the transition period
2. Stabilize the organization most rapidly
3. Strengthen the talent level in the organization
4. Reposition the organization to better serve the defined marketplace
5. Protect the bottom line

Activities that don't directly contribute to these five objectives are likely to be off target and a poor investment of time and energy.

Understandably, there will be some juggling and re-evaluating of priorities as the merger proceeds. But constantly changing priorities often creates the effect of multiple mergers, or a "one step forward, two steps back" scenario.

What helps most is to operate from the outset with a coherent, purposeful strategy, one that is complete with well-defined objectives and timetables. That takes discipline. But remember the truism: resources gravitate toward clear goals. A carefully developed merger integration strategy really pays off by giving you an excellent return on your investment of hours, energy, attention, and money.

# Be Bold.

**A**cquiring and merging an organization represents uncommon growth. The situation calls for uncommon management, bold stroke moves, a rejection of status quo management.

There are a number of phrases we frequently hear when companies describe to us the merger integration philosophy they are contemplating.

"We think we should move slowly...we're going to get it right the first time...we don't want to make any mistakes...we don't believe in knee-jerk decisions... it's important that we minimize the change."

Well, these are the wrong words. These ideas don't work. They reflect a conservative mentality that is highly inappropriate for transition management.

You've got to understand that when word of a merger leaks out or is formally announced, you've already lit the fuse on this thing called change. Problems are off and running. Top management can sit around the conference table believing in the weak wisdom of a careful, slowly paced integration strategy, but merger problems tend to set their own tempo. The cadence changes immediately, and astute managers will recognize this. Mergers often fail because management lets problems get way out in front, and then tries to play catch-up. It's the classic mistake, and these are the results:

1. Problems swarm on you.
2. Secondary problems develop.
3. You end up trying to put out fires, and a crisis management atmosphere prevails.

4. People start fighting symptoms instead of causes.

5. The management resources of the firm become overcommitted.

Once again, you simply don't have time to take your time. This is going to be the year of the two-minute drill, where decisiveness becomes the high virtue and caution becomes a curse. Allowing yourself the indulgence of a slow reaction time is positioning yourself (and your company) to be a victim.

"Change" is a wild horse you *have* to ride if you wish to control it. Just try to stay on it while it pitches and bucks. It won't grow tame merely by your standing outside the corral and waiting for some time to pass. And if you try to stand in its way, it will run right over you and drum you into the dirt.

We have a systematic assessment process called a Merger Management Review, and over the years we have used it to evaluate thousands of managers and executives when doing our *soft due diligence.* Our findings are very consistent: the best merger managers are those who are very *un*conservative. In fact, the best ones we've seen are more flexible than structured, more risk-taking than tentative, more aggressive than cautious, more decisive than deliberative, more creative than concrete in their thinking.

During a merger you need to become a bit of a gunslinger. There is real danger in waiting for problems to draw first…and you don't have the luxury of taking time to aim perfectly. We're not advocating that you proceed with wild abandon, but we do want to emphasize that the conservative, slow, methodical approach typically doesn't cut it in a merger environment. That can be the most reckless strategy of all.

# Put Dollar Signs on Decisions.

**A** merger is based on a financial proposition, a commercial viewpoint...it's not a "feel good" activity. Success is measured in numbers—dollars and cents, cash flow, net worth, stock price, marketshare, P/E ratio, debt figures, tax savings, and so on. It's a very digital issue. Your job is to help play the financial angles, to help deliver a bottom line characterized by black ink and big numbers.

Particularly during the early stages of a merger it's important to produce quick financial successes. That speaks volumes to the work force, because for a lot of those people the jury will still be out regarding whether it's a good merger or a bad one. If the company's financial condition begins to deteriorate, employees typically point to that as hard evidence that something about the merger was bad to begin with or is beginning to go sour.

So when you're weighing the alternatives in reaching your decisions, always take the financial angle into consideration. Almost always there are real dollars involved, even though that reality may not be particularly obvious.

It's very easy for companies to spend money on programs, benefits, or organizational changes that don't provide the appropriate payback. Also we have found that managers and executives in our client companies frequently fail to calculate the trade-offs of time for money. Part of our job is to hold people's feet to the fire so they adhere to a very tight integration time frame, because it gets very expensive when transition periods are extended. We constantly challenge recommendations and decisions where thousands...hundreds of thousands...*millions* of dollars are at stake, yet key managers have failed to run the numbers.

We also find that costly decisions are often made in management's attempt to generate goodwill. Companies are inclined to overspend in their attempts to buy loyalty, or to reduce feelings of guilt that stem from unpopular actions. It's much like overspending at Christmas—one or two gifts can communicate the thought, and additional presents don't necessarily provide value added.

Your employees will be just as concerned by what they perceive to be irresponsible spending during the merger as they are by harsh belt-tightening measures. They want the company to be fiscally responsible, not foolishly generous. They realize that their future is tied to the financial health of the new organization.

# Offer "Quick Impact Training" on Merger Management.

**M**anaging during the first year of the merger isn't going to be the same old drill, so the same old behaviors just don't offer a lot of promise. Executives, middle managers, and first line supervisors desperately need expert coaching on merger dynamics and how to handle transition and change.

This is no place for OJT (on the job training) or a learn-as-you-go approach. There's simply too much at stake. There are too many opportunities to foul up, and too much money goes down the tube when your problem-solvers and decision-makers are "playing it by ear."

There's little in the routine operation of an organization that would prepare managers and executives for managing this kind of corporate upheaval. Even the crusty, battle-scarred, seasoned veterans with years of experience under their belt can be rookies in this situation. It's not enough just to throw your A-Team at the merger if they essentially have to feel their way along. Undoubtedly they will give it their best effort, but it's like playing organizational Russian roulette. They may not get a second chance to make the merger work. At the very least, their learning curve is likely to lengthen the transition period at a point in time when additional days, weeks, and months are directly translated into lost productivity and hundreds of thousands of dollars down the drain.

So don't leave your management corps to operate in the dark.

• Educate them on what to expect, on what happens and why, when companies are being acquired and merged.

• Give them training on how to avoid the most common management mistakes.

• Show them the shortcuts to success.
• Give them a grasp of the proper priorities.

We argue hard for "quick impact training"–coaching that is intense, highly focused on the unique aspects of mergers, and rich in terms of specific "how to's." We also feel a key component of the training is to help managers reframe their personal job perspective.

People don't always realize they are paid to manage problems. In particular, they balk when confronted with a new set of problems that are merger-related. The management mindset must be:

> "I'm paid to solve problems, and to give the organization what it needs. If the problems are different now, that's okay. If the firm needs something different from me now, that's what I'll deliver."

Without proper training and coaching that give all parties a common frame of reference about merger management, managers and executives typically pursue conflicting strategies, argue over who's right and who's wrong, get in each other's way, and generally tangle things up miserably. A little bit of expert coaching on the front end, however, can bring the alignment of effort necessary for a well-orchestrated merger integration.

# Give Your Workforce a Proper Merger Orientation.

The merger transition period is marked by change, surprises, and ambiguity. Ordinarily that spells trouble, for three simple reasons:

1. Employees typically resist change.
2. They don't like surprises.
3. They're spooked by all the ambiguity and uncertainty.

So what's the best strategy for dealing with this dilemma? Meet it head-on. Prepare your people to deal with those things that cannot be avoided. Eliminate some of the surprise. Tell them about the certainty of uncertainty.

The key step in this process is to educate your people regarding the basics of being acquired and merged: how organizations are affected, the way people react, the difficulties that are to be expected, and how they personally can have a positive influence on the merger process.

When organizations fail to provide a proper orientation, employees feel like merger victims. They are much more critical of the way the merger is being run, and become alienated from top management. As time goes by you will see unnecessary damage done to the firm as morale erodes, turnover increases, productivity slips, and profits sag.

Employees find mergers less traumatic when they know what to expect. Also, when they understand the generic problems that just "go with the territory" during a merger, they are more patient and understanding when they witness management misfires, false starts, and mistakes. Instead of assuming the problems they see are unique, they will see them as the usual headaches all corporate marriages have in common.

So the proper orientation program is not only helpful to your employees, it also builds management's credibility and helps the organization as a whole navigate more effectively through the transition period.

# Take Care of the "Me" Issues.

The first word in merger is "me." Employees, first and foremost, are concerned about themselves as individuals and how they personally will be affected by the merger. *Their* top priority issues now are personal concerns, not company problems. These are the questions that fill the mind of the average individual:

"What's going to happen now?"

"Will I have a job?"

"How will my job change?"

"Who will I report to?"

"What's going to happen to my pay and benefits?"

Here's an idea you can take to the bank: people aren't going to worry about the company's survival until they are assured of their own. Your employees are not going to be very concerned about team play until they know whether or not they have a position on the squad.

Self-preservation instincts powerfully influence people's behavior and attitudes. Our merger studies indicate that fifty percent of all lost productivity during a merger transition period can be accounted for by employee attention and energy being diverted from work to worrying about the personal issues. An unbelievable number of hours get wasted every day, week after week, when employees are waiting on answers to the "me" questions.

It's management's responsibility to answer that burning question being asked by every employee – "How will *I* be affected?" Until the individual gets satisfactory closure on that very broad question, you're going to have only half an employee even though you're paying full salary. And, yes, that gets very expensive.

You also need to give your people reasons for wanting the merger to work. Selfish reasons. If they don't want it to work (because they feel they've been treated badly, for example), or if they haven't been given any reason to care one way or another, the odds of merger success take a nosedive.

We are relentless in pushing our clients to move with maximum speed in giving employees closure on the "me" issues. People can adjust to tremendous amounts of change, they can deal with disappointment, but they can't stand to be left hanging in the air wondering how they personally will be affected in the shakeout.

So don't design a merger integration timetable which implies that employees are a second priority. Also don't be foolhardy enough to think that your people are going to be more concerned about the company's wellbeing than they are about themselves, their families, and friends.

Don't ever forget it, the first word in merger is "me."

# Give Yourself Permission
# to Make Some Mistakes.

**M**erging companies is a complicated process. There is no school solution. So if you're afraid of making mistakes you'd better get off the dance floor, because in a merger you're going to trip over your own feet several times. (Plus, you'll step on some toes.) Mistakes are unavoidable when you're acquiring and consolidating organizations.

Let's face it–this is a risky business. The statistics of study after study bear this out, showing that the biggest percentage of mergers never really lives up to the dealmakers' expectations. But you certainly don't increase your odds for success when you concentrate on getting it perfect before you get into gear. Frankly, playing it safe is often the biggest risk of all. Prudence, beyond a certain point, becomes imprudence.

There is no such thing as a "zero defects" merger. In fact, an unwillingness to make mistakes is a fundamental error. It paralyzes you. Meanwhile, problems keep picking up speed. It's scary to watch how disaster accelerates.

You're going to be better off spending your time taking some chances, finding mistakes, and then fixing them. Essentially, the job of the merger manager is to seek and destroy problems.

We're not in favor of impulsivity or management foolishness. But we are devoted advocates of risk-taking. Problems are the price of progress, and they play a central role in the merger process.

So get with the program. If you make mistakes, admit them to your people and then get on with business. That's the way this game has to be played if you're going to have a prayer of pulling it off successfully.

# Keep the Focus on Clients and Your Marketplace.

**P**ersonal concerns fill the minds of employees during the merger transition period. They worry about how they'll be affected by all the change, fret over the myriad day-to-day aggravations, and commonly waste half the workday on unproductive behaviors such as gossiping, waiting for answers, or just being confused about how to proceed with their work. Overall, business suffers badly.

Clients and customers take a back seat, as employees are preoccupied with the internal affairs of the organization. Employees, from top to bottom, are more caught up in "looking out for old number one" than ever before. Customer service can really take a beating.

So merger shockwaves don't just bounce around inside your corporate walls–they are also bound to hit the people who buy your products or services. The clientele will be very sensitive to what's going on, and will actually start looking for changes. Just like the employees, your customers will scan the situation for evidence of whether they will benefit or suffer from the merger. Your firm is vulnerable, and the competition has an excellent opportunity to gain some of your marketshare.

Several steps are needed in order to mobilize your sales force and customer service groups:

1. Establish a DEW-LINE (Defense Early Warning) for rapid detection and reporting of any slippage in sales or customer service.

2. Provide a toll-free hotline for customers to call in questions, complaints, or suggestions.

3. Get physically closer to your clients–contact them more frequently,

and spend more time with them during those encounters.

4. Move rapidly to communicate the benefits of the merger, rather than letting the competition get there first with its side of the story.

Also there are a number of things you should do internally to encourage employee attention to clients and customers. Steps you can take to counter people's distraction and preoccupation with personal concerns would include the following:

1. Implement new service initiatives aimed at protecting (even improving) your firm's sales and service.

2. Give employees quick, accurate feedback regarding how things are going in sales and service.

3. Develop new merger-specific incentive programs that reward employees for high-quality performance during the merger transition period.

Everyone needs to remember that he or she is there because there is a business to run, not because a merger is taking place. And if they're getting paid to help run a business, that's what they need to concentrate on every hour of the workday.

# Make Everyone Responsible for Merger Success.

**A**ll employees need to get the message that, so long as they work for the organization, it's their merger. They don't have to like it…they don't have to believe it was a good idea…they don't even have to want it to succeed. But they're supposed to do everything they can, at their respective jobs, to make it a success story.

The merger is a monkey that belongs on everybody's back, not just top management's. So long as an employee is accepting a paycheck, he or she should assume mainstream responsibility for making a positive contribution on behalf of the merger. People can hate it, and feel like it's a bad thing for their careers, but they've got to support it. They have to promote it, energize it, and fix it when it breaks. If they're not willing to do that, they're supposed to leave because, frankly, they're no longer doing their jobs.

Can you imagine a football player saying something like this:

"That sounds like a mighty dumb play to me. The coach is stupid. Why should I help run it? I'm not gonna' run and block on a play like *this* one. I'm gonna' wander over to the sideline, get me a few sips of Gatorade, take a breather, and watch these other dummies try to score. I'll go back in when they're running a play I like. They never told me when they signed me up they'd be running *this* play!"

Obviously, you can't pull off a win when players have that kind of mindset. Everyone in the firm needs to have a make-it-happen mentality. But there are always some people who would rather sit on the sidelines and watch the merger fail. Maybe they feel disenfranchised, victimized, powerless. Perhaps rank-and-file employees, or middle management personnel, are polarized and feel distanced from senior management. Some employees may think (rightfully so) that their career or job satisfaction has been damaged by the merger, and they will feel blameful and vengeful. That's understandable...it's even acceptable. What's *not* acceptable is for those people continually to act like they feel instead of acting the way they're *paid* to behave.

Everybody needs to understand just how complicated the merger process is. Frankly, top management is not good enough to make it work by themselves. All people, from senior executives to first-line employees, need to be aligned and working in concert with one another.

You don't get this kind of support and alignment, though, merely by demanding it or ordering it. Likewise, you don't get it through a propaganda blitz wherein top executives throw a lot of "happy talk" at the rest of the company. Employees don't buy bull, no matter who is throwing it or how fast and furiously it's being pitched.

On the other hand, employees are remarkably good about rising to the occasion when you humbly ask for their help, and make it clear that it's desperately needed. They also respond when you show earnest respect...and empathy...and genuine appreciation...for their efforts in the face of the stress and struggle that goes with the merger.

So treat your people like valuable human beings, like adults, and be willing to lean on them.

Make every employee part of the merger posse. Deputize everyone. You'll be able to use all the help you can get.

## O R D E R   F O R M

# Smart Moves: A Crash Course on Merger Integration Management

1-20 copies       _____ copies at $12.95 each

20 or more copies       _____ copies at $10.35 each

Name _____

Job Title _____

Organization _____

Street Address _____

P.O. Box _____

City, State _____ Zip _____

Country _____

Phone _____

Purchase Order Number (if applicable) _____

Fax _____

Email Address _____

*Applicable sales tax, shipping and handling charges will be added. Prices subject to change.*

*Orders less than $100 require prepayment. $100 or more may be invoiced.*

☐ Check Enclosed     ☐ Please Invoice

☐ **VISA**     ☐ **MasterCard**     ☐ **AMERICAN EXPRESS**

Account Number _____ Expiration Date _____

Signature _____

## To order, call **800-992-5922**
### fax: 972-789-7900
email: http://www.PritchettNet.com/order
or mail this form to the address below

## PRITCHETT & ASSOCIATES, INC.
### 13155 Noel Road, Suite 1600, Dallas, Texas 75240
http://www.PritchettNet.com

# Management Consulting Services

Pritchett & Associates' global management consultants help clients successfully plan and implement large-scale strategic change. We've been improving the competitiveness of both large and small companies for over two decades—combining our knowledge and experience with an analytic, results-oriented project management approach.

Our consulting group will help you:
- Capitalize on new synergies during difficult merger and joint venture integrations
- Outsource processes/functions to refocus on core competencies
- Face the organizational challenges associated with the implementation of new information technology
- Redirect your culture to foresee and maximize strategic possibilities
- Create the architecture for continued success and competitive advantage

> **If you would like to talk to one of our consultants about your unique change-related challenges, please call us at 1-888-852-1250.**

# Training Programs to Implement Change

Pritchett & Associates' training programs build on the hard-hitting principles in our best-selling handbooks. These quick-impact, concentrated programs have been successfully used by organizations worldwide. They deliver a no-nonsense message on how to deal with today's rapidly changing business environment.

Our training programs will help your organization:
- Recognize the predictable dynamics of change
- Convert "change resisters" to "change agents"
- Improve operating effectiveness and productivity
- Shorten the high-risk transition period
- Keep people focused on the high-priority issues
- Restore stability and morale

> **Training programs can be customized for your organization. For more information, call 1-800-992-5922.**

## About the Authors

Price Pritchett is Chairman and CEO of Pritchett & Associates, Inc., a Dallas-based firm specializing in organizational change. He has authored more than 20 books on the subject, and has consulted to top executives in major corporations for two decades.

Ron Pound co-authored five books on organizational change and played a key role in the design and implementation of major change initiatives for a broad range of organizations, both domestically and internationally.

## Books by Pritchett & Associates:

* *The Mars Pathfinder Approach to "Faster-Better-Cheaper"*

* *Fast Growth: A Career Acceleration Strategy*

* *Outsourced: 12 New Rules for Running Your Career in an Interconnected World*

*MindShift: The Employee Handbook for Understanding the Changing World of Work*

*Resistance: Moving Beyond the Barriers to Change*

* *A Survival Guide to the Stress of Organizational Change*

* *New Work Habits for a Radically Changing World*

* *Firing Up Commitment During Organizational Change*

* *Business As UnUsual: The Handbook for Managing and Supervising Organizational Change*

* *The Employee Handbook for Organizational Change*

* *High-Velocity Culture Change: A Handbook for Managers*

* *Culture Shift: The Employee Handbook for Changing Corporate Culture*

* *Team ReConstruction: Building a High Performance Work Group During Change*

* *Teamwork: The Team Member Handbook*

*Smart Moves: A Crash Course on Merger Integration Management*

*The Employee Survival Guide to Mergers and Acquisitions*

*After the Merger: Managing the Shockwaves*

*Making Mergers Work: A Guide to Managing Mergers and Acquisitions*

* *Mergers: Growth in the Fast Lane*

* *Service Excellence!*

*The Ethics of Excellence*

*The Quantum Leap Strategy*

*you$^2$: A High-Velocity Formula for Multiplying Your Personal Effectiveness in Quantum Leaps*

New! Thought Leader Series:
Rapid-Read Handbooks

* *Leadership Engine: Building Leaders at Every Level,* based on Noel Tichy and Eli Cohen's best-selling hardcover from HarperBusiness, a division of HarperCollins Publishers.

*\* Training program also available. Please call 1-800-992-5922 for more information.*
*Call 972-789-7999 for information regarding international rights and foreign translations.*